# Journey on the Four Hills

G.R.G.M.

iUniverse, Inc.
Bloomington

iUniverse books may be ordered through booksellers or by contacting:

iUniverse
1663 Liberty Drive
Bloomington, IN 47403
www.iuniverse.com
1-800-Authors (1-800-288-4677)

ISBN: 978-1-4697-0062-5 (sc)
ISBN: 978-1-4697-0060-1 (e)

Library of Congress Control Number: 2011963519

Printed in the United States of America

iUniverse rev. date: 5/17/2012

# Dedication

To Rex, William, Celine, Ashley, Sierra,
Mitchell, Noel and those yet to come

# Contents

The First Hill     1

   The First Hill (Birth to Age Sixteen)     3

   Baggage of the First Hill     7

   Imprinted Gifts of the First Hill     11

   Value of Money     12

   Perspective     13

The Second Hill     15

   The Second Hill (Ages Seventeen to Twenty-five)     17

The Third Hill     25

   The Third Hill (Ages 26 to 59)     27

   Lessons Learned from My Third Hill     40

The Fourth Hill     65

   The Fourth Hill     67

   Notes to My Children's Children     68

   Rules for a Spiritual Life     69

   References     70

   Apache Blessing     71

# Preface

Each generation will make its own mistakes. I have made more than my share, but not everything that was imprinted or occurred was necessarily bad. Errors are an opportunity to learn. Imprinted errors are the challenges for which you have a life-time to overcome.

Here is what I have distilled in my life's journey. Some of it may find a home in your thoughts; much may not.

The "notes" are written with the hope that you will select those concepts that you can embrace, add your own, and pass them on to another generation. When problems occur, the "notes" may help you to understand them and work toward a brighter future.

# The First Hill

## The First Hill (Birth to Age Sixteen)

At the moment of your birth, you are born a perfect being. From then on, forces move you away from your "god-within". Due to genetic aberrations or congenital malformations, a few will be selected to carry an extra burden throughout their Four Hills.

You have little control over the damage imposed on the First Hill. The results remain with you for the rest of your life. Simply stated, you are under the yoke of others. Your likes, dislikes, and prejudices are basically the voice of others. You are being modeled by forces beyond your control and required to carry those burdens forward.

Only two forces truly sculpt your psychological and spiritual makeup: **Love** and **Fear**.

In their pure form, both Love and Fear are essential for your well-being. The flight-or-fight response of pure Fear is designed to safeguard your body. Love is there to assure your spiritual survival. Joy, interest, and the feelings of success and accomplishment are said to be allotropic forms of Love. Anger, hatred, jealousy, criticism, and egotism are said to be allotropic forms of Fear that have been corrupted.

Love is almost always creative. Corrupted Fear is destructive. Good and evil are just other words (code) for Love and Fear. Love and Fear play you like an accordion With Love you expand. With corrupted Fear you contract. Every action you take will borrow from one or the other, and sometimes both.

Our initial introduction to Love usually occurs over a nine month period. A mother's womb is the perfect world in which all needs are met. We have yet to be introduced to "I need/I want".

From the moment of birth, we are introduced to Fear. Suddenly, we are traumatically expelled from a warm, secure aquatic environment into a relatively cold environment in which things are done to us that, by their novelty and sometimes pain, constitute our first introduction to Fear.

Physiological needs never before experienced are encountered. The psychological consequences are molded from the balance between Love and Fear. Wants not met lead to frustration and anger.

As infants, we are dependent on someone for that which quells hunger and the need for body warmth that simulates the *in utero* temperature. Being initially powerless as a baby, too often Fear overpowers Love. The fear of not receiving, the fear of rejection, and the fear of disapproval are powerful. They lay the foundation for what is called the ego that we unconsciously construct to defend against these corruptions of Fear.

Criticism, lack of positive feed-back, rejection, and punishment are destructive to self-esteem and feed the need for the creation of the ego. Fears of rejection and of judgment fuel the ego's domination of your thoughts. We fear being judged inadequate or lacking. Sometimes we compensate through hubris. Hubris, false pride, is a manifestation of Fear. The failure of these needs being quickly and adequately met adds a new trigger to Fear. As our brains develop, new triggers to Fear are introduced when parental Love is misguided or absent.

Love and Fear are the foundations through which the biases of parents, peers, church, etc. find expression. Our impressions of the world, our likes and dislikes, the standards by which we judge others are not ours, but those of others imprinted on us. Without understanding it, we are reactive, not proactive to our environment.

**Fear has been the energy that created my character defects.**

Love is the greater force. Love is the light that permits us to expand. Receiving approval and praise builds inner confidence that you are adequate and worthy of respect.

I was blessed. My mother was pure Love; my father a somewhat darker shade of Love. Both were intelligence mixed with kindness. Nevertheless, the more dominant force in my life has almost always been Fear. It created my dark side and counteracted my desire to reach out for love or express love.

Using the standards imprinted upon me, my ego had me being judgmental of others to counterbalance the fear of being inadequate. As a child, we are a vehicle for implanting thoughts that create differences between yourself and others. Intellectual pride, love of possessions, snobbism, need to stand with those who are powerful, etc. are merely responses to Fear. When I asked God for relief of a problem, I was unconsciously acknowledging my lack of control. To the degree that I did not escape my initial indoctrination, Fear caused me to contract who I could be. Only Love allows your escape from the imposed prison of Fear and expands the breath and quality of your life.

*"... He that feareth is not made perfect in love." (1 John 4:18)*

Without truly nurturing care-givers, you are going to be damaged. Other individuals character defects will impose on you burdens that you will bear on your life's journey.

My journey across the First Hill was not gracious, but it was well buffeted by two outstanding parents. Not until my Third Hill did I fully appreciate their wisdom. At the age of eleven, smoking and drinking became game pieces in my attempt to fit in. I remember vividly my parents calling me into the living room. On the table were a carton of Lucky Strike cigarettes and a bottle of Johnnie Walker black label scotch. They told me that I could smoke and drink, but only in front of them. Both tobacco and alcohol went on a long sabbatical. In college, I experimented with a pipe but for reasons that had nothing to do with tobacco.

My parents were dipoles. My mother was a beautiful, elegant (both physically and spiritually) outgoing individual, who saw the world with amazing clarity. When my parents gave large parties, I would come down to a place on the stairs where I could watch the on-goings. After the party, she would ask me what I thought of certain individuals. Like most kids, I could read an individual's dark side What always amazed me was that she would then take my observations and their presumed implications well beyond my initial impressions and then restore dignity to the individuals negatively judged by identifying their positive virtues.

My father was a man of relatively few words. When he spoke, everyone, and I mean everyone, listened. More often than not, his words were recognized as wisdom by others: significantly less frequently by me. I learned to listen the hard way. I was a very stubborn child. Challenges to his authority were met with three explicit warnings and then the belt. The hits were those that left welts on my back. The hand had to merely go to the belt for me to recalculate my intended course of action. In all fairness, I never received a punishment that I did not merit.

## Baggage of the First Hill

My first big problem was hair. My mother loved my curly black hair. She allowed it to grow too long. "What a cute little girl" did nothing to promote self-esteem. Finally, at age three, the locks found their appropriate resting place on a barber's floor.

My second big problem involved language. My parents spoke French. Their friends spoke French. Even the doorman of the building spoke French. When I went to pre-school, I was shocked to discover that no one spoke French. I never again spoke French until I courted my first wife some twenty-five years later.

My third big problem was my name, Gilles. I hated my name. It was readily confused with Jill and presumed to be a girl's name. The similarity did not pass unnoticed among my peers.

My fourth problem was my lack of acceptance of my physical self. I was tall and lanky. Most of my classmates were shorter and thicker. The soot of my discontent extracted a heavy price for expectations not met. The negative implications did little to build self-esteem.

My fifth big problem was that, even though I was born in the United States, I was in essence French. Being French was not good. Germany had just defeated France. Neither did little to enhance communal acceptance, particularly from two brothers who lived across the street. The younger of the two was a year older and twenty pounds heavier. He found pleasure in fighting with me almost on a daily basis. I did not complain to my parents, but when the results of one such encounter became evident, my father told me, *"In any fight, there is not a winner and a loser. There are two losers. Make certain that he knows that he has been in a fight."* When I broke his nose and did something to a tooth, the fights ended. This event coupled with the feeling of being an outsider fed my dark side. Fear of being rejected or attacked tapped into my gene pool. Rather than wait for a possible fight, I would walk into the school yard, pick someone out and start a fight that I intended to win. In grade school, I spent a lot of time in the principal's office. After a while there was no need to fight, but the two loser concept was deeply engrained in my psyche.

My sixth big problem was that I had dyslexia (7 plus 6 = 31). Back then, no one knew what dyslexia was. In the fifth grade, I tested out as mentally challenged. That is polite language for retarded. Little in the way of intellectual demands were ever imposed until an older teacher in the seventh grade took me aside and, in a very stern tone, told me that I was probably the smartest child in the class and needed to start performing to my potential. This was the first of two educator-based interventions that shaped my subsequent intellectual development.

My seventh big problem was the family history. Every other generation had produced a leader. Here I was, a kid who had had to fight almost daily to combat his fears and who had been told by his school that he was a mental retard, being informed that he was obligated to become a leader of God knows what. An unwanted torch was placed in my hands. I doubted that I could ever even pick it up much less carry it.

My eighth big problem was my high school. Rather than allowing me to continue in public school, my parents sent me to a preparatory school. St. Paul immersed me into the prevailing male peer skill sets constituted by sports and dating. Being a European, my father did not understand the role sports play in determining societal status within the American educational system. For him, most sports were a waste of time. My social assimilation into high school was compounded by money. St. Paul was a school for rich kids. My family was not poor, but my father's concept as to how wealth needed to be handled made me poor. My father gladly paid tuition, books, etc, but anything beyond a small allowance was not a valid consideration.

Being a first generation American translated into my trying to be an American and a little something more. In elementary school, I had played some softball and that was it. In high school, acceptance meant playing football. St. Paul's Preparatory School for Boys presumed that everyone who could afford its tuition could buy the required sport gear. I used my allowance for helmet, shoulder pads, jersey and shoes, but lacked funds for pants. As a consequence, I was allowed to practice, but not play in a game until the pants were purchased. Knowing that I was good enough as a freshman to start on the junior varsity team did little to lessen my resentment.

The money for the pants came from being a busboy or dish washer at the local inn. At least once on the weekend, I could be assured that I would have the privilege of dealing with a school mate and his date. My father had previously ingrained in me constructive channeling of resentment-based aggression. Quoting someone whose name I have forgotten, *"If you can control it, aggression and anger can become a power which can move the world."* In my case, it was beating guys who outweighed me by sometimes fifty pounds. Football was a perfect outlet. It was elementary school all over; only this time I didn't have to go to the principal's office.

My parents never came to see me play. That was probably in my best interest. Some of the things I did would not have met with their approval. Playing football was therapy for me and a big problem for the guy on the other side of the ball. My intent was to inflict pain. That ended up being a two way street. In my senior year, I broke my leg.

Academically, my marks improved significantly, but at a price. Being a dyslexic, it took me three hours to do the work that my classmates could do in an hour. St. Paul was a boarding school. Lights out occurred at 10:00 p.m. sharp. My dating money was significantly compromised by having to buy lots of flashlight batteries. Under the bed covers, my homework got completed. Love and respect for my parents drove me under the covers of my bed in an attempt to fulfill an imposed obligation. Fear of not being accepted drove me into sports.

My father had traveled extensively in his life. He had visited Russia twice and had witnessed the transformation of Russian society. He foresaw the impending clash that he termed class warfare. Determined that I should possess a skill set either in my hands or head, he decided that I should focus on becoming an engineer. The thought of building inanimate objects did not thrill me. From that day on, I did as poorly in mathematics as I could get away with. My academic deviations from expectations promoted my parents to have me undergo two days of "aptitude testing". The tests confirmed that I would make a lousy engineer, but they allegedly revealed that I had a very inquisitive mind and would do well in medicine or the sciences. That was fine with me. Anything but being an engineer. When I ultimately enrolled in college, it was as a pre-medicine candidate.

## Imprinted Gifts of the First Hill

**Religion**: Superficially, my religious upbringing was as unnatural as it could be. My father was Muslim and my mother was Jewish; yet they meshed perfectly. They both rejected the separation that their respective religions imposed. Decades later, I finally understood what they knew: all there is to true religion is summed into the first two words of the Lord's Prayer: "***Our Father .... .,***".

Religion was the one thing my father schooled me on. He was a great admirer of the ethics embedded in religion, but considered formal religions as corruptions that created states within states. He imposed his bias indirectly by telling me that "*God is like the essence of all creation that resides at the top of a hill. There are many paths up to the top, but beware of he who tells you that his is the only pathway up. What is important is that you make the journey*".

For him, heaven was the attainment of a spiritual relationship with God: definitely not a place where the physically dead are warehoused. Not until my third hill did I understand what a gift I had received. He prepared me to accept that the blood of an Israeli is no more valuable to God than that of a Palestinian, that the blood of a white South African was no more esteemed than the blood of his or her black brethren. Without this understanding, there would have been a significant barrier in any pathway to a spiritual life.

My parents obliged me to take a religious odyssey. I attended Catholic mass, Hebrew classes, served as a Lutheran choir boy, attended Bahai camp, received my bible from the Congregational Church, and attended an Episcopalian prep school, a Quaker college, and a Methodist medical school. Only the Quaker and Native American philosophies of life found a place in my religious consciousness. While on my odyssey, my father asked me only one question: *"If Christ were to revisit this world which religion would he embrace as being most in keeping with his teachings?"*

When he died, I witnessed men physically fight for the right to be his pall-bearers. There were to have been four. He was carried out by eight: two Hebrews, two Muslims, three Christians, and a Bahia

In my life's journey, a man's race or religion was not a barrier when we met.

## Value of Money

Because of my father's professional expertise, as a boy I attended most white tie-and tail openings at the Metropolitan Museum of Art. Despite our middle class standing, my mother had a personal magnetism that drew her into the upper echelon of New York Society.

My father was fair, but at the same time, tight with money. He had respect for wealth and contempt for its misuse. He viewed money as a tool that one needed to use carefully. *"It is good to be rich. It is bad to act rich"*. For my father, money's primary purpose was to assure one's freedom. What you don't do is *"You don't buy loyalty, friendship, or love."*

He was very aware of wealth's destructive dark side *"When wealth accumulates, people decay"*. Father's idea of what money was intended to achieve was very pragmatic: *"You do not need a Rolex to tell time. The sun and the position of the stars do a good job. You don't need a fancy car to get from one place to another."*

How you will use wealth is an indication of where you are in the balancing act between Love and Fear. Christ threw the money lenders out of the temple. Today, we compensate them when they move away from their god-within. We do things to "preserve our way of life" without being sure that it's God's way.

> *"Money never made anyone rich"*.
> Seneca

## Perspective

My father asked a friend, T. C. Lu, to take me on a tour of his store of Chinese antiquities. His store was a miniature Guggenheim Museum before the Guggenheim was ever built: a twelve foot balcony filled with works of oriental art spiraling upwards for five stories. As I leaned over the topmost balcony railing looking down at an immense Buddha that dominated the first floor, I heard him say in a tone meant to be heard: *"Occidentals see the world in term of decades; we Orientals view the world in terms of centuries."*

In the Chinese scrolls and paintings, the individual is but a small figure eclipsed in the greater landscape. In Western art, figures are portrayed as full bodied or half figure with the background subjugate to the personage. Who we are and who we think we are lack a meeting place.

My first hill was done with neither grace nor dignity. If I could have chosen, I wouldn't have picked being me.

# The Second Hill

## The Second Hill (Ages Seventeen to Twenty-five)

Loaded with all the baggage from my first hill, this was the most difficult of all hills to travel. Love from the family had been overshadowed by outside peer pressures that fed deeply into my dark side.

Imprinting had defined my prevailing beliefs. Coming from a European background, the way I saw things did not necessarily conform to the prevailing norm and did little to allay a sense of being an outsider. I used being judgmental to compensate for the fear of not being an American in America. Judging became my ego's building material for a façade of arrogance that insulated me from the fears encountered. I deprived those being judged of their underlying worth and dignity.

My second hill has its parallel in the story of the butterfly. At this stage, I was very much the caterpillar. Standards set by others were not initially met for the simple fact that I was not prepared, physically, intellectually, and emotionally, to run a hypothetical mile in a specific number of minutes.

Failure in not succeeding occurred more often than I care to count, but my real failures were in not trying to take the opportunity to succeed or fail. I did not try to heal the wounds nurtured by my fears. Rather than viewing not succeeding as a triumph of overcoming Fear, my ego had me repress my failures and store them in the subconscious to do ongoing damage. Too late on the Second Hill did I understand that failure is success if we learn from it.

False pride is a powerful tool in the hands of the ego. The ego tells you, *"Don't try, then you cannot fail"*. Recognition of a deficit or weakness in others gave me a pseudo buffer to the implied fear of the situation. In the battle for respect of self, the dark side often won until I changed my perspective as to what was failure. To succeed in the Second Hill, I had to learn that every conflict unsuccessfully addressed needed to be viewed not as a failure, but as an opportunity to take a negative experience and heal my exposed weakness in order to make the future more fruitful.

Not being comfortable in my skin permitted envy and jealousy to assume too much influence on the second hill. Jealousy is an emotional explosion in slow motion. On my second hill, I did not understand that *"until I was grateful for what I am and have, wanting more was adding a burden to an already weakened foundation"*. I wanted so badly to be someone other than me.

Despite my dyslexia, I had performed well academically in preparatory school, but to do so required my putting in significantly more time and effort to be competitive with my better school mates. Dyslexia forced me to solve challenges in a way different from my peer group. Because retention of factual knowledge was difficult, I learned to analyze why the fact had to be. Despite terrible SAT scores in English, somehow my headmaster engineered my acceptance into the number one small college in the United States, Swarthmore. In hindsight, this was a life changing event.

My name got changed. In high school, Gilles came out in six to seven variations. At Swarthmore, when asked my name at registration, I took great care to carefully enunciate my name. When I saw the white of the lady's eyes and heard a confused *"what?"* I quickly replied, Richard. For four years, I was known as Dick.

At Swarthmore, I expected to be asked to go home at any time. My classmates were either number one or two in their class or gifted in other ways. Convinced of my inferiority to them, I reverted back to targeting to get just a passing grade.

In my junior year, I was exposed to an exceptional teacher who fired my interest in his course. On the mid-year examination, he told the class that the grades ranged from a C minus to an A minus. Then he added that he had given the A minus to the individual to tell him that he could do even better. As he handed out the corrected midterm tests, I silently prayed for a C and not the C minus. I got the A minus.

Once I knew that I could compete on a high level, I received one of the two top grades on either the mid-term or final in almost all the courses in my major. A second intervention by a teacher had altered the course of my journey. A true teacher inspires and exposes the path to a brighter future.

Each subsequent success built respect for self, but also fueled a bit of my dark side. I now enjoyed challenges and even sought them out. Calm water did not always remain calm water. Like a child with a new toy, I played. Successes built a sense of false pride that further insulated me from my Fears.

I had played football and attempted baseball in high school. At Swarthmore, no one except freshman females took football players seriously, and even they quickly outgrew their jock itch.

Football came naturally, not because of great talent, but rather because I had learned to take my resentments out on the opposing players. At Swarthmore, reputedly the best place to watch football games was under the bleachers. Playing football and especially JV football was not a big deal. Despite weighing 160 pounds, I played defensive end. I had sufficient three step quickness to get by most opposing tackles. With the other J.V. defensive end weighing 198 pounds, little wonder what the second or third play from scrimmage was. Ultimately, we played a number of teams composed of coal-miner's sons. Spending significant time with my face pressed into the grass educated me as to the need to find another outlet for my aggression.

Determined to play baseball, I worked hard at improving on my marginal high school skills and did just that. In my freshman year, I played first base despite being described as someone who was in danger of being killed by a thrown ball. I could hit and batted in the number three or five position until my eye-sight changed. Sheer determination, not talent, allowed me to play for one year with relative distinction on the J.V. college level.

In teaching myself to play baseball, I was privileged to witness a great example of grit winning over talent. The person in question was a short, thin, nerdy looking engineering student who wanted to be a goalie on the lacrosse team. If you don't have lightening-quick reflexes, goalie is one position you don't want to play. That winter, while I worked in the gym at addressing my shortcomings in baseball, he would work out throwing that little, black rubber ball at a concrete wall and having it come back at him at lightening speed. I was convinced he was going to seriously hurt himself. His body stopped almost as many balls as his stick.

At Swarthmore, it was easy to get on a team, but not necessarily ever play. He did not make the lacrosse team until his junior year.

That year, he never played in a game. In his senior year, the prior varsity goalie had graduated. It was anticipated that the JV goalie would take his place. That never happened. After the second game, he became the varsity goalie. If it meant stopping the ball with his teeth, he did what others were not prepared to do. When the season ended, he was selected as goalie on All-American Lacrosse team: the same team as Jimmy Brown (whose football jersey I had transiently touched in a high school football scrimmage).

Ultimately, the message penetrated. My Higher Power never intended me to play sports. I stopped trying to be a prototype American male clone and focused more on self discovery and dreams.

I had an extraordinary girlfriend, Jean who is still a good friend to this date. She was one of three great women that I have had the privilege of knowing. She re-set the academic bar which served me well in medical school. She was perceptive, intuitive, and nurturing. The male brain does not attain its full potential until age twenty-four. In college, I still had years of growing up and left without her.

As I progressively learned to respect myself, I had more time for dreaming. Dreaming is one of the most important functions for being a successful person. Kinetic power resides in true dreams. Without dreams, we tend to vegetate meaninglessly as paying spectators in a make-believe world created by mass-media and others.

My marks improved considerably. At graduation from Swarthmore, I was the pivot between the upper half and lower half of my graduating class. Given the talent exhibited by my classmates, I was thrilled not to have graduated in the bottom half.

Baggage from my past became as asset in a contorted way. I was rebellious against authority or concepts that I perceived false. When I went to medical school that posturing got me into trouble. I was black-balled from the National Medical Honor Society by a professor I had seriously offended. Though I succeeded in pissing off a few of my teachers including the dean, I impressed others who had greater standing.

By my sophomore year in medical school, my brain development should have been nearing its completion. My girlfriend was the most impressive female that I have ever met. She was Swedish. Her father was a world famous professor of mathematics and head of the Mathematics Institute at Princeton. In addition to beauty and intelligence, she had the quality of being a nurturer. When a decision was required, one more time Fear ruled. Her intellect was so dazzling that whoever married her would, by necessity, have had to walk two steps behind her. Years later, when we got together again, she had four children and I had four children.

By my senior year, my companion was a very bright, attractive young lady from Wellesley. She too was great, but her manipulative skills grossly overshadowed her nurturing skills. I likened the relationship to that of a lion trainer and a tigress. It required going into the relationship with a chair and whip in hand to keep things on a level plane.

At graduation, the dean pulled me aside and told me that I had done something that no one else had done except number one students: take a position in the top ten and never relinquish it.

He finished his comment by saying *"I almost mentioned it"*. He didn't need to. Successes in medical school fortified the hubris of my dark side.

By the end of the Second Hill, the load of baggage had been lightened, but still weighed heavily.

1. The transition from self-loathing to self-respect was accelerating.

2. I was still an outsider. Except for women, I still sought out talented friends at the fringe of the main stream.

3. Hubris (one of my ego's defenses against being deemed inadequate) interfered with the development of humility. I continued to use aloofness as insulation to keep all but a few at a distance. The ability to see through to the core of an issue and be correct fed the arrogance that was a band-aid to my underlying feeling of inadequacy.

4. Having accepted my dharma and modified it to embrace a concept of service to others, I was in a hurry to fulfill it. I lived too much in the future to the detriment of the Now.

5. The ability to see solutions had another negative component. I learned at an early age to analyze problems in terms of the worst possible outcome and prepared mentally for a compensatory course of action. In my senior high school year, I achieved

two conflicting distinctions. I was voted the class pessimist by my classmates who did not know me and class optimist by those who did know me.

6.  My godfather's counsel to *"reach beyond what was attainable"* was just beginning to take hold. The last part of his admonition was *"otherwise what is heaven for"*. I had no idea what he meant by heaven.

7.  My endorphins came from doing. I forgot to smell the flowers, and take time out to "play hard".

# The Third Hill

# The Third Hill (Ages 26 to 59)

**The Third Hill is the battle ground of life**. Here is where I needed to rid myself of the imposed baggage of the first Two Hills and the defects of character fashioned by my ego.

The goals on the Third Hill are simple:

1. Find out who you really are.
2. Who you can be.
3. What is your dharma?
4. Live your dharma.
5. Be excited about the mysteries of life.

Don't sell out for what is transitory and not based upon spiritual values.

Cicero once wrote *"If you don't want to come to old age with bitterness, you must early perceive what you want to do and not get sidetracked by illusions of living".*

Sir William Osler wrote *"Live as if there is no tomorrow and as if tomorrow is forever".*

Wayne Dwyer wrote of not living a life half-lived. *"Don't die with your music still inside". When you die, what do you want to be remembered for?*

The only one true four-letter word in the English language is "Why?" (the question mark is the fourth letter). "Why" often brought me to confront the limits or shallowness of my knowledge.

It forced me to acknowledge my ignorance and in so doing imposed some much needed humility.

If you come to believe in a Higher Power, dharma is something to honor. To make life meaningful, try to align your dharma with service. In your quests to answer the challenges in front of you, use imagination and insights from within. In committing to medicine, my pathway to service was direct. I thus circumvented the trap of serving a poor master, namely me.

The key to my Third Hill was achieving respect, if not love, of self. Love of self is very distinct from self-love which usually masks self-hatred. To do this, I had needed to find the means to counter the negative forces of the first Two Hills that had eroded my self-esteem and sense of self-worth. The Third Hill was more about unlearning the emotional burdens I brought there than it was of learning factual knowledge.

Acceptance of myself lessened the need to be aloof and distant. It rendered me safer from the opinions of others. I was better able to be true to myself whether others liked it or not. My acceptance of self helped to save me from the bondages of Fear and ultimately opened me to have greater compassion for others

An early step on the Third Hill was embracing my name. Four years of Richard/Dick was enough! Being American meant now being me. In medical school and beyond, my name was Gilles. If a professor or classmate had a problem pronouncing it, I was patient, but persistent in assisting them. Later when science took hold of my dharma, my professional publications and books bore my two middle initials. The family tradition has been that males bear as middle names the first names of their respective grandfathers.

When you learn to accept yourself honestly, you will have taken a critical step toward changing the course of your life for the better. How you deal with adversity will determine in part your success.

Some of the difficulties I encountered were self-imposed. A growing sense of self respect coupled with the analytic process developed to counter dyslexia allowed me to periodically challenge prevailing opinions. How you make another confront conceptual error is an important second to being correct. Too often, I focused on winning the battle and not on doing so with compassion.

The biggest problems were usually imposed through third parties. The work done at the National Institutes of Health laid the foundations for my academic career. Ultimately, I was recruited to what was to become over a ten year period one of two best departments in its area of specialization in the United States. Everyone was a peer on a very high level. Success breeds resentment. When the department's chairman left to become Vice Chancellor at Penn State, fueled by envy, the other departments chose a self-centered prodigal son who had no idea of what it was to be an academic father. The chairman's paranoia about the success of others became a destructive issue. I learned a valuable lessen from the situation. Because of their established academic reputations, departmental members looked the other way when the chairman began attacking individuals within the department. Within four years, the most talented individuals, including myself, had left.

Leaving fueled a new level of creativity. When a somewhat similar situation occurred for a second time, I again significantly profited from the move. I have come to believe that these individuals were inserted by a Higher Power. In a strange way, I am grateful to them.

Adversity is there for a purpose: that purpose being to prepare you for next stage. Difficult situations are opportunities to learn to develop the necessary skills to flourish in the tomorrows. *"When things get tough, the tough get tougher".* Be strong!

The lead shoes of yesterday are the works of Fear. Regret of what should have or did not happen are destructive to self-respect and diminish the power of the Now. Regrets and resentments occupy valuable space that robs us of the magic and creativity present today. Like cancers, they grow into the spaces of tomorrow. You have to let go. In forgiveness and especially self-forgiveness, I found a release of energy that nurtured my spiritual growth.

> *"To escape from the traps of the ego, wear the shoes of today. Each second that passes will not come again."*

**Gratitude:** Gratitude is a healing force. Learning to have gratitude for even the simplest benefit was one of the great gifts received on the Third Hill.

Too often, I had looked at the glass-half-empty and not at a glass-half-full. Often I overlooked the gifts embedded in seemingly negative events. When I would go to a fishing tournament, I pulled my boat with my old blazer SUV. One day after returning from a tournament in which I had done well, the radiator decided to permanently retire. Its replacement was expensive, but that did not bother me. I was filled with gratitude that the event did not happen the previous day, thirty miles from the nearest town and that I had been permitted to savor the tournament's outcome.

There is immense serenity in gratitude. Near the end of the Third Hill, I finally understood that gratitude was the true prerequisite for spiritual meditation.

**Prayer:** I was never taught to pray, but somehow always felt compelled to get on my hands and knees every night and attempt to communicate. But when things went wrong, I found my self trying to bargain with God for things or outcomes desired.

In the words of Forrest Gump, *"Stupid is as stupid does"*. If I believed in a Higher Power and its intent for my life, why was I now asking for intervention to change it?

On the Third Hill, I finally understood that praying was never to be about asking. Prayer is for thanking God for my children and attempting to bring me closer to the god-within that resides within each of us.

Meister Eckhart wrote *"If the only prayer you ever said in your whole life was 'Thank you' that would suffice."*

**Attitude:** What you think colors the entire day. A negative attitude contributes to darkening whatever transpires. If I got up out of bed with a piss-poor attitude, the rest of the day was colored gray. A negative attitude is a destructive fire whose soot affects those around it. How you start the morning is how you'll see the day. Start the morning with your gratitude list. It will recolor your thoughts.

Attitude is both inward and outward. Outward is our behavior; inward is where we are in our journey towards a more spiritual life. Somewhere it is written that *"you should treat people as if they are worthy of your best behavior"*.

**Tolerance:** The *status quo* is not life. Rivers do not stand still. The air we breathe is never the same. I had great trouble with the defenders of the *status quo*. I saw creativity trampled in what I visualized as being the *"sewers of unimaginative minds"*. For this, I totally lacked the gifts of tolerance and forgiveness. My journey would have been easier had I exhibited tolerance and compassion and not been such a threat to the possessors of a zombie mindset. I failed to confer to those that I held in contempt the dignity of being a fellow human being. In so doing, I forgot the old Persian proverb: *"A fool has nothing to learn from a wise man, but a wise man has much to learn from a fool"*.

What I was slow in realizing was that my negative opinion of another individual usually mirrored some fear within myself. I thought being an alpha male was part of maturation. Little did I realize that all my macho posturing was a defense by my ego to deal with the implied threat potentially posed by another individual.

Through academic and social successes, respect for self grew. It nurtured my self-confidence so that I did not need external affirmation.

**Choosing:** Having been raised in a European home, I unsuccessfully attempted to reduplicate the imprinted domestic pattern. My father ruled everything outside of the house; my mother everything within.

The relative merit of my understanding of women is reflected in the poor final choices I made in selecting life-long partners. Let me correct the statement: by accepting being chosen as their respective mate. All three of my wives made the decision well before it was effectively communicated to me. The decision to ultimately unite in an intimate relationship usually does not reside with the man. Just look what happens in nature. The male builds the nest, struts, etc., but it is the female who makes the decision: witness the short, bald millionaire with a trophy wife. He desired; but she chose.

In choosing a mate-for-life, do what I suggest and not what I did. Avoid individuals who are narcissistic or lack nurturing skills. Excessive self-love is but a cover for an insecure individual with little room for others in his or her personal equations. Narcissism destroys the ability to achieve true intimacy between two individuals.

Women and men achieve decision making through different channels. For survival of the species, women, and not men, are genetically primed to be the more valuable of the two sexes. Answers to most complex questions have already been addressed in nature. With a few evolutionary exceptions in which the passing of physical strength is important to species survival, the female has been the selector of what genetic characteristics need to be chosen. Survival of the species necessitates that selection skills reside with the female and that the period over which they function be prolonged. There are differences in skill sets between men and women and the timing of their availability.

**Males & Females:** The unisex brain is theorized to exist only transiently. The female brain is the model from which the male brain undergoes testosterone's rewiring. The release of the sex hormones determines the way the brain functions. Testosterone appears to negatively affect the areas of the brain dealing with communication and emotional sensitivity while enhancing aggression and order. With their communication and emotional centers left intact, females are better at reading faces and hearing emotional voice tones.

Females reach puberty earlier than males. At puberty, girls are taller relative to boys of the same age and more advanced in their social skills. Female brain maturation is complete at age 17; whereas the male brain reaches maturity about age 24. When you compare a 17 year old boy and a 17 year old girl, the differences are glaring. The impulses for mating, bearing and rearing of young are evolutionary traits hardwired into the female brain. If survival of the species was primarily dependent on the male, given his proclivity for aggression, the human species, more likely than not, might have long been extinct.

By the act of giving life, a female is naturally creative. Both males and females have had limitations placed upon pursuing their dharma. A male's creativity has traditionally been exchanged for the need to sustain and economically protect the family. Fulfillment of so doing does not alleviate the individual need for creativity which, if unmet, leaves behind a spiritual void. Men, by their very nature, have a need to be creative and to be appreciated.

In the grand design, the male's role has been to be the physical provider, protector and genetic contributor. That the male was intended to be expendable is clearly reflected when one goes pheasant hunting. If a hen and a rooster are close together in bushes, guess which bird your dog is on point for and soon to be dinner.

As a male, I found it difficult to reach out for help. Males are supposed to "tough it out". These concepts had an imprisoning effect on accessing my emotional capital.

**Controlling**: Other than my hubris, my attempts to control were a way of dealing with my guilt about having subjected your parents to a narcissistic destructive mother in their formative years and having stayed in a bad marriage too long. In over-compensating, I did not allow them the freedom to take responsibility for their own actions and to experience the consequences. That coupled with my ego's dark side, hubris – thinking I always knew what was best for them, I impeded their development. For that, I am truly sorry. I did not know when to let go. I became an enabler rather than a healer. In trying to force solutions, I created resentments that could have caused residual damage. Some call it "*wintering of the heart*". I have had to forgive myself for so doing. I did not praise their achievements enough. More often than not, I would point out the next hurdle to overcome or mountain to climb at a time when they needed time to catch their breath. By so doing, I impeded their personal growth. I had and still have great difficulty detaching and letting go. Detaching with love is an art form that has eluded me.

We all have the impulse to control. Why? For me the answer was Fear: fear of the possible outcome.

> *"He who controls others may be powerful, but he*
> *who has mastered himself is mightier still."*
>
> Loa-Tzu

**Judging:** The mind that attacks is responding to Fear and not Love. Negatively judging others is part of my dark side. My fears created my need to identify flaws in others in an attempt to elevate my perception of self. Having a strong military linage did little to temper an aggressive posturing. That imprinted or genetic quality spilled over into dealing with individuals that my ego found wanting or disliked. I did not necessarily view weakness or character defects with the required compassion. My warrior's mindset reinforced my childhood fear of being inferior. A well-adjusted individual has little need to look for flaws in others.

The bible speaks of *"Judge not that ye be* judged". We judge for fear of being judged. Being judgmental is to counteract some underlying fear. By judging others, I could confer to myself a sense of superiority. It took me a very long time to understand the fear of being judged had fostered in me a need to see others in a less favorable light. It took an even longer time to learn that judging clouded my perception of the true essence of the other person. Judging imprisons us in world of false interpretations-confabulations of reality. When I judge someone, now I ask what my reaction says about me. Judging is one of Fear's contractors.

The blame-game is a corrupted form of judging. Deeming someone more at fault than another was my deflecting guilt stemming from my partial culpability.

**Anger**: Anger is Fear being threatened. It is a cry for protection.

It's easy to let anger find its voice. The desire to punish or retaliate dominates. Once driven to anger, I usually had lost control. When something ignites an angry response within me, I found the anger to be due to selective interpretation of somebody's action that touched deep fears within me. Instead of responding immediately to the anger within, ask yourself "why"; why am I angry? If you are honest with yourself, you will expose a wound unhealed.

Anger is simply me out of control. It is not unlike a run-away vehicle. The emotional wound touched is in position to cause additional damage. Being immersed in a cloud of steam and soot, when I attempted to punish someone, I often ended up hurting myself. The consequences were usually long in coming. When you let anger rule, you are conferring victory to your presumed adversary.

When I got better control of my emotional explosions, I often found that I was responding to something out of proportion to its true status.

Anger is like a drug that feeds our perception of being self-righteous. Properly channeling anger is the first step towards forgiveness. Make anger constructive, not destructive.

**Hatred:** Hate is an extreme separation of you from your god-with. It is an ugly form of defecation on self.

Always look for Why. As a child, I was programmed by my heritage and the mass media to hate Germans. It was not until the Second Hill that I comprehended how manipulated I was so as to deny universal brotherhood.

**Regrets/Revenge:** Revenge is a bummer. In its naked form, revenge is a hateful form of grief for something in the past. The transient satisfaction from achieving it does little to off-set the cost of attaining it. Unachieved regrets and revenge are energy consuming vehicles that profit no one and hurt you. Negative thoughts over which I had poor control from a resentment would drag me down

The Bible states *"they know not"*. Revenge has been described as *"the poison you take, thinking that it will hurt others"*. I had to dig down past the resentments I felt justifiable and find the darkness in myself that caused them to flourish. This was something I would try but often pulled back out of fear of what I was discovering. The insanity of these thought occupying lesions forced a journey's end.

Both regrets and resentments are ongoing destructive attitudes. I needed to purge myself of the underlying toxic ideas. My record on being able to do so was not perfect. What helped was the often repeated saying: *"If you pursue revenge, dig two graves"*.

To free myself of the bondage of the anger fueling either resentments or regrets, I knew that I had to learn to let go. Knowing and doing are not always on the same page. Until I opened my acceptance of a Higher Power, I rarely had the ability to truly let go. Letting go involves forgiving. With forgiving comes a rush of positive energy.

*"An eye for an eye leaves the world blind."* You do not need to look at the current global conflicts to understand the wisdom in Gandhi's statement.

Somewhere in a twelve-step book is written *"it's not men's actions that disturb us as much as it is our reaction to them"*. The power of resentment is destructive.

**Envy:** On the first and part of the second Hill, envy was present. It took a long time for me to understand that envy is a waste of time. It took my appreciation away from what I had. Gratitude for what I had had been put on vacation. Envy created a subconscious resentment that separated me from those I envied.

Envy is jealousy's younger brethren. Jealousy and envy are hostile forms of self-pity. Their antidote is gratitude. Envy is a non-lethal poison, but it is a poison nonetheless. A little can be beneficial, but a lot consumes valuable positive energy. "I want" is only three steps removed from "I'll take". You have only to turn to the Old Testament to read the stories of "I want/I take" that are varnished by a thin coat of justification.

**Jealousy:** Jealousy is another name for heightened envy. When called by that name, you recognize that you are dealing with a "green-eyed monster". If there is a more valid standard, direct your energies to achieving it rather than craving it. Don't compare yourself to others. There will always be someone spiritually better, smarter or more attractive. Focus on where you are in your quest for a spiritual life and be grateful for being there and not at St. Elsewhere.

**Expectations:** Expectations have often been for me well and sometime not well intentioned applications for resentments. Failure to achieve the designated objective built up resentments.

## Lessons Learned from My Third Hill

On the Third Hill, I pursued my dharma, but at the same time, I needed to survive emotionally, physically and in other ways. To physically survive on the journey requires money. The Third Hill taught me the dangers associated with money. The words of my father found a second voice. **Money is there to create freedom:** the freedom from want, the freedom to choose, the freedom to physically move, but most important, the freedom to have convictions. Abraham Lincoln wrote: *"To sin by silence when men should cry out makes cowards of men"*.

Most individuals lack the financial buffers to be true to their moral or ethical convictions. In T. H. White's 'Once and Future King', the boy Arthur asked Merlyn *"Why do people not think when they are grown-ups as they did when they were young?"*

In a world whose prevailing god is green, most individuals must disassociate their spiritual and ethical idealism to the pragmatics of survival and in so doing destroy their dreams and dharma. I had to learn the hard way that having "fun" needs to come from a spiritual reservoir, not penetrate from without. Spiritual wealth is not green. When individuals die, their material toys do not come with them, but spiritual gifts may.

**Authority**: Authority gives someone the power to be a leader. Authority does not make him or her a leader. When I met a true leader, I tried to reason out the whys. Let him or her be an educator. A true leader usually creates an environment that supports individuals to be what they can be.

You do not have to always obey authority, but you must respect it. We now live in a world where right is not necessary might. More simply stated: *"A 45 automatic beats four aces every time"*. Individuals who resort to authority/force as justification for what they do are exposing their failure to lead.

**Politics**: Politics is the pathway to power. Power is the corruptor of those who seek it. *"Nothing corrupts as completely as power"*. In time, a politician can become an individual sucking his or her *id* with little regard for what is around him or her.

If gifted with intelligence, individuals get to choose between creativity and political astuteness: rarely both. The short-cut to power is being politically astute: translated, developing the art of ass-kissing and ass-covering. These individuals are dangerous to those with creativity. They understand the first law of mediocrity: *"If you cannot compete with a standard, destroy it"*.

One of my three biggest problems on my Third Hill of life was the belief that creativity or being right would win the day. I was often wrong! Nevertheless, I survived individuals with brown noses and obtained political power while still being creative.

Attainment of political power tends to be a two step phenomenon. First, you need to gain entrance into the inner circle and second, get their attention through a combination of creativity and political astuteness. You cannot reverse the order. If you get their attention before gaining entrance into the inner circle, the embedded brown noses will identify you as a threat to them and make your entrance difficult.

In seeking political control, be careful of its corrupting nature. Read and re-read *The Hobbit*. The user of power will always be diminished by the use of power. You can exhibit strength, but avoid resorting to power unless absolutely forced. If that moment ever is forced, let your adversary experience its consequences. Wounding a lion is not in your long-term interest.

**Mediocrity**: My not being blessed with an excess of tolerance and possessing a paucity of humility created significant challenges. Nothing threatens mediocrity more than someone or something that challenges the *status quo* and mediocrity's embedded position within it.

Be careful of mediocrity. It's a potentially powerful force. If allowed to grow within an organization, it first becomes an obstructive influence. If allowed to expand to a critical mass, more than blasting power is required to dislodge it.

Historically, we crucified anyone three standard deviations from the mean. Currently, we assassinate the few who dare be one standard deviation removed from the mean.

When referring to this world, the comedian, Morrie Brichman, is quoted as saying: *"I'm scared! I don't know whether the world is full of smart men bluffing or imbeciles who mean it."*

**Buying Things**: The Third Hill has taught me is that often my need for luxuries or for having "the best" were coverings for emotional voids that have not healed.

Again, I find myself echoing the words of my father:

a) Don't confuse luxuries with necessities.

b) Buy things whose price and quality will serve you well without pushing you into economical servitude.

c) If you don't need it, don't buy it.

d) If you can't afford it, don't buy it.

e) If you buy it, take good care of it for it has cost you hours or weeks of your life.

When you buy something on credit, the bank owns you. Try and make that period of economic servitude as short and painless as possible. Do not become a hostage of things. Economic slavery is something we choose to do to ourselves.

My wants and desires did not always have a solid foundation. Their genesis often resided in my being immersed into today's mind-controlling technology. The world projected through television is not reality; but like Pavlovan dogs, we buy into it. Ultimately, the piper must be paid. Do you remember the story of Pinocchio? He and two other children are invited to overindulge in having fun and eating treats. In time, they are transformed into donkeys. Rather than being served, they become the servants of those who own the amusement parks.

Somewhere in the late eighteenth century, materialism gained widespread acceptance in the everyday lives of Americans to the point of challenging foundations of religion and ethics. Darwin's law of natural selection was advanced by the privileged as justification to rationalize their behavior. Individuals adopted a Nietzsche-like doctrine of self as being the center of something approaching worship. To the phrase *"all men are created equal"* was added *"but some men are more equal than others"*. Today, Judeo-Christian ethics have been hijacked by Madison Avenue. Belief in the ethos of materialistic consumption has become cornerstone and pillars to the temple dedicated to "moi" (Miss Piggy's use of the French word for me). Add-ons are portrayed as necessities and material things as pre-requisites required for emotional and social stability. Materialism is an addiction that corrupts the human soul.

The move from one state to another helped to advance my education as to the value of "things". When forced by necessity to re-evaluate my possessions, the amount of "pseudo-necessities" that made their way to the Salvation Army or trash was sometimes both impressive and liberating at the same time.

**Committees**: Periodically, you may be asked to sit on committees. When you serve, try to remember why committees are created:

a) As a mechanism for warehousing a problem until it auto-resolves or progresses to crisis and

b) As a mechanism to buffer those who may be forced to make an unpopular decision.

If the person creating the committee had really wanted the problem solved, he or she would have remembered that *"God so loved the world that he did not send a committee"*. If ever on a committee, take your charge seriously, less a less competent or manipulative individual replace you.

**Being Interviewed:** Whether for a job or a television show, the rules are the same. You are there for a reason: to tell a story. Don't wait for someone to ask you questions. Prepare several one-two minute (by the clock) presentations that describe your perspective as to why you are there and what you have to offer and insert them into the conversation when the opportunities present themselves.

Country music has been described as a three minute soap opera. In an interview, you are the singer.

**Education**: In my attempt to fulfill my dharma, I was thrice blessed in that I could **serve** by being a physician, **educated** by virtue of being in academics, and as a researcher, **answer** some of the whys?

Education is simply the attempt to translate facts into experience and action. We tend to call the transmission of facts teaching. Too often, students become so inundated with facts that they literally drown, never having appreciated the underlying basic concept behind the facts. Good teaching is often reflected in the ability of the student to formulate and ask an intelligent question.

The best quality of a teacher is the ability to arouse enthusiasm in a student so that he or she will learn. The art of teaching is the art of asking questions that resonate within a student. Imparting information is not teaching; to inspire and challenge is. There is a bonus to teaching: *"A teacher effects eternity"* (Henry Adams).

Teaching opened doors in my mind that had been previously shut.

In today's society, too often we are becoming readers and observers without understanding what we observe. Emphasis is too often focused on factual training rather than analytic thought.

> *"The true product of education is that which is*
> *left after all factual knowledge is lost."*

Education is learning a way of thinking that is transportable from one area to another and by which we develop a deeper sense of questioning of ourselves and our world. The key element of education is to stimulate imagination. Imagination sustained by experimentation becomes genius.

Be careful of the cost of education. Loans are easy to obtain, but they are difficult to pay back. Student loans hold the recipients in perpetual economic bondage. When possible, minimize the amount of your indebtedness. Debt is a form of enslavement and a killer of dreams.

**Research:** Research is the art of asking imaginative questions and the quest to answer the four letter word, **Why?.**

Innovation is often a disruption of the *status quo*. New ideas make the guardians of past knowledge feel uncomfortable or inadequate. Louis Pasteur best summarized the problem when he wrote: *"New revolutions of thought, even those imposed by scientific demonstration, leave behind vanquished ones who do not easily forgive or forget"*.

Research is being a Trekie. The scientific mind is that of an optimist. Imagination is a common denominator of great scientific minds. The essence of science is putting questions to nature. There is little difference between the imagination of a good scientist and that of a poet except the mind of the scientist is that of an optimist.

*"It is not possession of knowledge that makes a man of science, but rather the persistent and relentless quest for understanding."*

Science is the attempt to bring order out of diversity. The real question is whose order is being sought. Albert Einstein said *"I want to know God's thoughts, the rest are details"*.

The underlying order to the universe speaks to the existence of a Higher Power. When I was confronted with problems in science or in morals, I'd look to nature and indirectly to its Higher Power for the answers.

In his early days, Louis Pasteur was a very good water-color painter. He even contemplated making his living by painting. He had the ability to absorb fragments and to synthesize them into a unified concept. He had faith in the natural world that allowed him to jump from g to z and be correct. The lack of this faith is sometimes reflected in an unwillingness to venture beyond the next step without documentation of the knowledge embedded in that step.

*"Solutions come to minds that have prepared to receive them. Scientists do not solve problems, they perceive God's solutions."*

**Technology:** Technology is the two edged sword that ultimately cuts the wrong way. We need it for national prosperity. We need it to prolong the privilege of life. But machines do not have a god-within. They capture their masters and render them less competent. Give a young child a calculator and his or her ability to do simple mathematics is impaired and ultimately lost.

Improperly used, technology is eroding that fragile concept we call humanity. Jobs lost through technological advancement will not come back. Without the dignity derived from work well done, one is slowly dying despite a daily breath. Respect technology, but be aware of its power to destroy. A former president of the United States once said:*" The test of our progress is not whether we added to the abundance of those who have much; it is whether we provide for those who have little".*

There is an even darker side to technology. The flesh-and-blood community is being eroded by the newly created virtual community. With technological mastery comes isolation of the soul.

**Choosing a Vocation:** Try and make your avocation and vocation the same. The allure of wealth is a false god. If humanly possible, avoid the money traps. Do something that you enjoy doing that has the potential to sustain your humanity. Working for but a paycheck is but a form of robbing yourself.

You may have no other choice; if so, do as my godfather told me:

*"Do what ever you have to do as if unto God."*

The rest usually takes care of itself.

Pragmatically, most individuals are forced to abandon their dharma in order to support a family. There is a very short window of opportunity in which you can explore whether your dharma has the potential to provide you with a living. Don't waste that precious time.

Success usually is achieved by the most persistent. Have a plan for your life and be patient. Try to understand where today's action will lead your plan. By so doing, what is irrelevant or tangential will become apparent.

One warning: *"Do not do on Friday what you did on Monday."*

Grow your skills. Be open to new ideas and respectful of old ones.

**Employment:** There are certain rules which will make you successful or unsuccessful in your job.

1.  If you work for someone, you are part of a team.

2.  No team can work efficiently, if one member lets the soot of his or her discontent contaminate the work place.

3.  Always look for ways to improve your job skills and productivity. My godfather tried to teach me two things:

    a) Never accept your limitations.

    > *"If we accept our perceived limitations*
    > *and do not reach for that which is thought*
    > *to be beyond attainability, then,*
    > *what is heaven for?"*

    b) Do all things, no matter how menial, as if unto God. Booker T. Washington wrote:

    > *"No race can prosper till it learns that there is*
    > *as much dignity in tilling a field as in*
    > *writing a poem."*

4.  Always present yourself and your work in the best light possible.

5.  The employer expects you to be loyal, courteous, respectful, and honest.

6.  In doing all this, remember to sell who you are and what you represent, but do so with dignity. You need to do so for no one else can.

Being principled in your actions mirrors what is inside of you. These are simple rules when you work for someone.

Ultimately, try to be your own master and guide your destiny.

*"You will never be as well served as when self-served."*

**Problems:** You will experience problems: some small that are easily forgotten and others that are definitely more memorable. More simply stated *"shit happens"*. When it does, what just happened is not a Now issue; it's already in the past. What you do with the problem is the Now issue.

Focus on the solution and not the problem. Understanding the individual elements of the problem gives you the potential for bringing an answer to the problem. Being in the problem and worrying about it is often a prayer for what you don't want to happen. In one of the twelve step books is written: *"Worrying is payment for a debt that you do not owe"*. Get your head around the problem and give back that part that is not yours.

*"Problems are either stepping stones or stumbling blocks, depending upon how you use them."*

**Idle Time:** Time emancipated from obligations has been for me very, very special. Creativity is often born out of boredom and solitude.

Boredom within idle time was a necessary step for my being creative. Someone pointed out that water left alone stagnates. Don't let excessive idle time be destructive. We are bombarded by external and internal noises that compete for our attention. The greatest noise of all is silence. Kick the voices competing for your attention out of your head and seek solitude of mind. Use idle time for dreaming your dreams and pursuing them. Whether successful or not, it does not really matter. The quest of dreams makes up life. Their attainment is anti-climactic. Don't sell your dreams and spiritual values to drift comfortably in the midstream of being.

> *"To make great dreams come true, the first requirement
> is the capacity to dream; the second is persistence."*
> Cesar Chavez

**Words:** *"When you are speaking, you're not listening."*

Words are very powerful. They can either hurt you or hurt others. Like bullets, once spoken they will do their damage. If you intend to hurt, use them with full realization that their consequences will be lethal to that relationship now or at a future date. Words once said can never be fully retrieved. It is best that you not spend your emotional capital ransoming back statements that inadvertently slip from your tongue. Be careful about the words you use.

When words hurt you, look for the reason why they hurt. They have usually touched an emotional void or a residual pain burden.

Lies may anger you, but they do truly hurt. If you can find the courage to bring to consciousness why a word or sentence causes pain, you will minimize their ability to hurt you as intensely in the future.

*"Sticks and stones may break my bones,*
*but words will never hurt me"*

Eleanor Roosevelt is quoted as having said:

*"No one can make you feel inferior without your consent".*

There is a time to keep silent and a time to speak. Before speaking, ask yourself, "do my words create or destroy". My mother recognized my tendency to be blunt. She would tell me *"Turn your tongue over in your mouth three times before speaking an unkind word"*. I have often spoken words of criticism without understanding their potentially destructive force. Periodically, destructive words unintentionally separated me from others, but more importantly from my God-within.

*"The stroke of the tongue breathe the bones"*
Ecclesiastics

**An Open Mind:** Be open to new ideas. Receive them as you would a stranger in need of shelter, but do not embrace them as friends until they have proven their worth. New ideas are revolutions. They threaten the tenets that they propose to displace.

What is new is not necessarily right. Only if challenged and confirmed, should their contribution assume its rightful place. Remember that what we embrace as The truth today is little more than error up to date. Be careful of the ideas that you guard. They can become ruts in the road of your journey. Be sure that the rut is never so deep that you cannot change directions. Beaten paths are for beaten men and presumably beaten women.

**Moving Mountains**: It is said that one truly motivated individual can move a mountain.

The rules are simple:

1. have a dream,

2. enroll others in your vision, and

3. create a brightness of the future for that vision with believable alternatives.

**Love:** On a personal level, Love is my most difficult subject to reflect on. Having long sheltered my emotions, to do so is pushing the envelope far. I have traveled to summits in medicine and science, but, in being intimately in touch with my emotions, I have lived in valleys of denial.

Giving love and accepting love do not come from the same source. When my children went to summer camp in Georgia, a lady named Jane Mack taught them a song whose words have since became etched in my consciousness: *"Love is the only thing that given away will bring you more."*

Love is the great expander of relationship with our fellow human beings. Another word for love is kindness done with compassion.

In a strange way, giving of love is like the giving away money. Love without strings attached, without conditions or expectations. Let your Higher Power determine the rest. The gift to you is having experienced the powerful emotion of loving. Loving with expectations is a formula for resentments.

Accepting love was and, to a degree, is still a problem for me. I feared to completely express love for in doing so, I exposed my vulnerability. Fear has prevented me from reaching out and caused me to imprison my instincts in the fortifications built by my ego. Giving love comes naturally, but accepting love still requires a long ladder. This is an area where Faith has not completely conquered fears

Some forms of love are purely cerebral; other forms have a hormonal foundation. The Chinese view love as a form of insanity. They counsel those so afflicted to wait until the insanity has passed. Only then, if both parties concur, should the union be sanctioned. Go slow! Break all the bed springs necessary. Be sure of your feelings. Time is a good judge of the validity of your choice.

If you are in doubt as to whether someone cares for or loves you, try applying this test that a very special lady once told me: "*You'll know the people who love you by the things they do that cost them personally.*" Recognize the difference between crumbs from an overburdened table and actions indicative of sincere attachment.

**Loaning Money**: You create a destructive barrier between the two of you when you loan a friend money. Expectation of its return may engender occult resentment rather than thanks. Either say no or give it away with no conditions attached.

**Gifting**: If gifting comes with no expectations or conditions, it is beautiful. Gifts used in the hope of obtaining a desired objective are in a less noble category.

Pragmatically, what males do not understand is that women do not function under the same ground rules as men. There is no such thing as "pay-forward" in the female playbook. The anticipated impact of big expensive gifts is grossly over-estimated. For women, any gift influences only the now. Tomorrow is a new day that carries with it a clean slate.

Women, like men, need reassurance of their being loveable and loved. Great rewards can come with small expressions of affection. Instead of expensive jewelry, cars, etc., court your chosen with cards, poems, symbolic gifts, flowers, candy etc. Frequently, expressions of love will have longer impact than a few costly gifts.

Don't try to buy the affection of a woman unless she puts a for sale sign out.

**Giving**: Giving shares aspects with Gifting, but it is more fundamentally allied with Love. It is all about the underlying state of mind. Most giving comes with expectations. Often my giving had strings attached or was *"crumbs from an overburdened table"*. I had to learn giving in two steps. The first involved removal of all expectation; the second when possible, finding pleasure in the acts being anonymous.

Having once lived in the rural South, there was a type of giving that I came to greatly admire. It embraced a sense of humanity. One time, I was fishing an isolated stretch of a river and ran out of gas. Ultimately, a boat came along and towed the boat back five miles to the landing. By doing so, they almost themselves ran out of gas. I tried to refill their two tanks. They refused. It was an unspoken, pass-it-on. After that I would near always stop on a country road when someone broke down. When asked *"What do I owe you?"* the answer was the one that I had been taught: *"Nothing"*. Unconditional positive acts lay a foundation for spiritual progress.

**Marriage:** Given that I am on marriage number three, this is a subject that contains a significant amount of *"do as I say and not what I did"* within it. The alternative is more salt that you could carry.

Avoid making my mistakes. In seeking a partner look for:

1. A person who has genuine respect and concern for you

2. A person that is a nurturer.

3. A person that can grow with you or independent of you

4. A person that you enjoy breaking bed springs with.

5. A person that has caring parents.

A girl borrows from the father, but copies the mother. Understanding the inherited family dynamic will prepare you for the future.

Whatever is presented during the courtship is probably the best you will ever know. The person you court or are courted by and the person you marry will differ. In courting, both you and your beloved have modified your behavior to accommodate the other. Neither of you consider these modifications to be permanent. Once legal bonds are in place, you both tend to revert back to your pre-courtship posturing: convinced that you can modify your partner. I thought that I could teach my first wife to redress her addictive, self-consuming tendencies. Wrong! You can never change anyone, but yourself. No matter how many coats of dye, a tiger is still a tiger and a skunk is still a whatever. The words "I do" have triggered some interesting transformations as witness my second wife.

Before we got married, my third wife asked me if I could accept her the way she was. I answered "You could stand some fine tuning". She busted out in laughter. "I'm glad you didn't ask me that question. I already had planned what I was going to change in you."

Marriage creates a situation in which to achieve union, both parties have made a compromise from an ideal mate. The true definition of a compromise is two unhappy individuals. Until the illusions of the unattained are extinguished, it can be argued that all marriages are conceived of in hell and not heaven.

The first year of a marriage tends to be an S-shaped curve. You start with enthusiasm and high expectations and then aspects of personality previously underappreciated surface. New responsibilities take their toll and you slide down the S. But the S has an upswing. How high your travel on the up-swing is what your marriage will be. From the very beginning, if you both can agree to accept the other person as they are and are honest about it, you'll have less resentment.

It took me years to fully comprehend why my parent's marriage worked so well. My mother executed her manipulations with respect for my father. She wore velvet gloves. Only once did I ever see them come off.

**Friendship:** True friends are your family-of-choice. Treat them as well, if not better than blood family. I have been blessed in having five true friends. If I were ever in trouble at three o'clock in the morning and called them, I could hang up the phone with complete confidence that they would be there shortly.

In my case, my friendships have outlasted marriages. Men usually forge friendships in the fire of a bonding event. A separation of time does little to minimize their sincerity.

Treat friendships as if they are a garden. When watered and fertilized with Love, it will bear you great gifts. True friendships have deeper roots, but even they need periodic nurturing.

**Journeys of Silence:** I had to learn to make a special time for myself and to use mental ear plugs to drown out the voices in my mind that competed for attention. Try to close your mind to external concerns in order to open it to meditation.

*"If you don't have time for meditation, you'll*
*have lots of time for life's crap."*

Mediation has been described as an application for serenity. To be able to meditate, you must first learn to control your thoughts.

Separate your thoughts from the past, now and future. Attempt to identify what God is thinking. True silence is serenity that comes from kicking all voices, but that of God, out of your head.

There is a dark side to silence. Silence based upon sullenness, self-pity, and self-loathing is silence from the dark side. Silence with any trace of anger or hostility loses its power and speaks as destructively as words. Sulking silence does communicate, but the wrong message. It is pouring oil on troubled water. Not infrequently some has a light.

Make silence an ally, not an enemy. Try and reason out the other's destructive behavior and then look at what your reaction to it says about you. That is never an easy question to answer.

> *"There is a time to keep silent and a time to speak."*
> Ecclesiastics

**Gratitude List:** I took a lot of things for granted, and, in so doing, lost access to joys that came from the many gifts in my everyday life. Until you attempt to identify the gifts embedded in the day, you miss out on their uplifting power.

Learn to do a gratitude list at very least once a week, better daily. The cup is really half full, not half empty. Use prayers only as a time to communicate with your Higher Power. Give thanks for the gifts you possess.

Gratitude is a tool for changing attitudes and behavior. Always give thanks for the privilege of a physical tomorrow. Enjoy what each day brings without apprehension about tomorrow.

Gratitude translates into service to others. *"A person who lives, but in the service of self, serves a dark master".*

**Democracy**: This article published in Daily Commentary says it all:

> *"A democracy cannot exist as a permanent form of government. It can exist only until the voters discover that they can vote themselves money from the public treasury. From that moment on the majority always votes from the candidates promising the most money from the public treasury, with the result that a democracy always collapses over loose fiscal policy followed by a dictatorship. The average age of the world's great civilizations has been two hundred years. These nations progress through the following sequence: from bondage to spiritual faith, from spiritual faith to great courage, from courage to liberty, from liberty to abundance, from abundance to selfishness, from selfishness to complacency, from complacency to apathy, from apathy to dependency, from dependency back to bondage."*

This thesis is said to have been written by Alexander Tyler when the thirteen colonies were still part of England. When the Supreme Court allowed unlimited political contributions by corporations, it effectively doomed America's experiment in democracy. Now, big business can fund ad lib the candidates that do their bidding.

You will have to deal with a nation mired in selfishness and not far removed from complacency and apathy. It is only a question of time before we have a single governing party and ultimately a single ruling family. Our nation started as an oligarchy of rich men. Today it is an oligarchy of powerful corporations. What the purpose of any form of government?

*"The purpose of any government is to convey wealth from the public sector to a privileged private sector."*

**The Revolution:** Women have been physically and economically suppressed. Fueled by militant feminism and their increasing economical and political power, women are now creating a dynamic metamorphosis of American society from a male-dominated, patriarchal society to a matriarchal one. Protection from employment discrimination, inclusion in affirmative action, abortion law reform, access to contraceptives, right to initiate divorce, right to own property, greater representation in media, universities, professional institutions, school athletics, near pay equalization, gender language changes, and control of their own sexuality are examples of the re-addressing of prior social inequalities among the sexes.

In the past, a man's economical status in the world had been determined through comparison, contrast, and competition against other men. The consequence in the delay in brain function maximization was not yet to be significantly in play. A seventeen year-old male could have the relative luxury of being able to be immature and underperform as his comparison, contrast, and competition (the three destructive Cs) were measured against only other brain-underdeveloped males. The seventeen year-old female is sexually and intellectually more advanced at this point in time. At seventeen, important decisions are being made as to who is selected for college and at twenty-one, who is selected for medicine, law, veterinary medicine, pharmacy, etc. The male becomes competitive too late in the selection process. The males that do compete successfully come primarily from other cultures.

Women will continue to progressively displace men from positions of both power and wealth. The radical transformation marked by the economical liberation of women, supported by the ascent of women into positions of power and the age advantage of maturity that women have over their male counterparts, will create an imbalance between the sexes relative to acceptance into professional academic institutions. Once in power, women tend to preferentially choose other women until they understand that the sex that they must fear is not that of men.

The gap is not an intellectual one, but one of maturation timing. My oldest son, Rex is an example in point. In high school, he may have gone through the cheerleaders of three schools and distinguished himself as being second string All Nebraska soccer goalie. Academically, he was somewhat above average. Things did not improve greatly in college. If I had not interceded, dental school would have been out. Once he hit twenty-four, he has been lights out. He chose service over private practice; became the best dentist in the Public Health Service; revamped dentistry for Native Americans on reservations, became leader of the regional dental unit in the Army Reserves; designed what is now the U.S. Army's mobile dental clinics; received a medical of commendation from the Army (something rarely given to someone in the reserves) for designing the mobile dental clinics now used by the U.S. Army. He has been twice cited in the Congressional Record for his innovative work with Native Americans, etc... .

Men are late bloomers who have longer staying power. Late bloomers stay the course longer and truer. Women have a number of detracting influences that ultimately shorten their time in employment bondage.

*"Occidentals see educational problems in terms of a
decade or two and not in term of centuries."*

Unless the so-called education geniuses of this country divorce themselves from test number game, at sometime in the future, they will cause a truly destructive change in American society. The primary fiscal support of the family may well become the responsibility of women.

The psychological impact of this role reversal is going to be significant. As the male feels himself progressively disfranchised from a meaningful role in the family structure, the emotional fabric of the family may become strained. As stay at home fathers, males will be hard pressed to fully develop the nurturing skills that are naturally embedded in women. The implied consequences for emotionally strong and stable families are not promising. One parent families may become the norm.

There is a potentially darker side to the role reversal in American society. Historically, *"the only thing the oppressed truly have ever learned from their oppressors is how to be a better oppressor"*.

**Family**: A tight family is difficult to economically exploit and emotionally destroy. Divide and exploit is today's fiscal game. Commit yourself to a unified, caring family or be prepared to ultimately stand emotionally alone. A family is the choice of two individuals; its success requires genuine mutual commitment.

**Formal Religion:** By virtue of marriage or choice, you'll be pressed to embrace a splinter group of one of the three prevailing western religions.

To me the concepts of heaven and hell are religious code for Love and Fear that is used by formal religion to control. Similarly, sin and sinners are relatively modern day rhetoric used by the church to achieve a similar goal. Neither saints nor sinners exist, only individuals whose distance from their god-within varies. There is no devil anymore than there is a bogyman that will punish disobedient children. The devil is just a mind-control symbol.

Among those who profess a true commitment to Christian ethic, the Amish impress me the most. Their church is not one of bricks and mortar. Their church is the community.

The essence of true religion is **Love**. That of formal religion incorporates Fear. My father's words have an echo in these thoughts.

# The Fourth Hill

# The Fourth Hill

On the Fourth Hills, your choices are to wear out or rust out.

*"Even if I knew that tomorrow the world would go
to pieces, I would still plant my apple tree."*
Martin Luther

In World War II, the famous French writer, Jean Paul Sartre was a member of the French underground. His cell was betrayed to the Germans. He and his fellow resistance fighters were lined up against a wall. The Germans began systematically shooting each man. A young German officer recognizing Sartre pulled him out of the line two bodies in waiting short of where he had stood. Sartre was to write of this event that he did not really start living until he had accepted the certainty of his death. Living means embracing the Now: not the day or hour, but the very second before you and before, like Sartre's comrades, it is no more.

The Fourth Hill is a more tranquil challenge. It is a time of letting go of dreams as yet unfilled and immersing oneself in the gratitude for those fulfilled. With no more Hills left, ignoring the failures of the past is a challenge. In your journey, you will try many things. Most will fail; but you will be remembered for your successes.

In my remaining journey, I intend to enjoy its special challenges and gifts. At its end, I hope that "my spiritual cup will be full" and *"the music will not have died inside"*. Through my work as a physician and researcher, I have served my dharma. Now, I need to work on the distance between myself and my god-within. In so doing I will need to wear the shoes of the Now and purge the clutter in my mind and the baggage from my previous hills to attain serenity.

I have lived a life corrupted by **fear** that has blinded to its workings in defining my character defects. My life has been bent by many fears that often never truly came to pass. I have lived with my love imprisoned by the fears imposed by the first two hills of life.

## Notes to My Children's Children

*"The words of a father must skip a generation to be heard."*

Use your character defects, like anger, jealousy, judging, etc. to identify your fears. Within you resides the courage to confront them: *"reach beyond what you think is attainable"* in seeking the Light.

On their journey through the Four Hills, all humans are blessed by the love of a Higher Power. In the words of Antoine de Saint-Exupery, *"Look to yourself to learn the meaning of life"*.

When asked *"What is heaven?"* My godfather's answer was *"Heaven is when your actions are in the service of God."*

Where is heaven? Christ answered it when he told us *"The kingdom of heaven is within you"*. It is for you each to find the way to your-god-within.

You are in God's hands. My greatest hope is that each of you will reside in a safe harbor with a nurturing individual.

I am truly blessed in having you in my life.

## Rules for a Spiritual Life

**John 4:16** *"God is love; and he that dwealth in love dwelleth in God and God in Him."*

You were born with God within you. That essence is always there. Whether you seek to reunite with your god-with-in or not, the choice is yours. If you so desire, here is my cheat-sheet to refer to if and when you get lost.

**Identify your dharma and live it.**
**Practice daily meditation'**
**Speak and act as if unto your Higher Power/God.**
**Live in the solution and not the problem.**
**Let the godwithin you be involved in your daily life**
**Walk with serenity and light that comes from the God-within**
**     that binds your humanity to that of others**
**Live life in service of more than yourself**
**Make your life count for something**
**Have creative dreams tempered by humanity**
**Develop the strength, discipline and imagination**
**to seek out those dreams**
**Money's function is give you the freedom to**
**make individual choices**
**Seek to be in harmony with nature**
**Build a great journey without fearing.** *"The best dreams are forever".*
**It's the journey, not the end that counts.** *"The road to God is always under construction".*

> *"To die but not perish is to be eternally present."*
> **Lao-Tzu**

To do any portion of the list requires discipline. Try reading the daily message out of an Al-Anon book (*Courage to Change* or *Hope for Today*). Make your gratitude list. Then, kick all the allotropic forms of Fear out of your mind and seek in the resulting silence a voice from within. Failure to do so would tell me that I was programming myself in the wrong direction.

> *"When you were born, you cried and the world rejoiced. Live your life in such a manner that when you die the world cries and you rejoice."*

> Old Native American saying

## References

If you read only four authors in your life, consider:

**The authors of the Bible, Koran or a comparable work chosen for you by your heritage Emmet Fox, Eckhart Tolle, Kahlil Gibran**

**P.S.:** There is one additional little book that helped me better understand my Four Hills: *The Little Prince* by Antoine de Saint-Exupery. Before beginning a new Hill, re-read it again. The words will be the same, but their messages will change as you gain insight and wisdom.

# Apache Blessing

May the sun
bring you new energy by day,
May the moon
softly restore you by night,
May the rain
wash away your worries,
May the breeze
blow new strength into your being,
May you walk
gently through the world and know its beauty all the days of your
life.